ANCIENT CIVILIZATIONS

A DAY IN ANCIENT ROME

by Janie Havemeyer
illustrated by Cesar Samaniego

Tools for Parents & Teachers

Grasshopper Books enhance imagination and introduce the earliest readers to fun storylines and illustrations. The easy-to-read text supports early reading experiences with repetitive sentence patterns and sight words.

Before Reading

- Discuss the cover illustration. What do readers see?

- Look at the glossary together. Discuss the words.

Read the Book

- Read the book to the child, or have them read independently.

- "Walk" through the book and look at the illustrations. When and where does the story take place? What is happening in the story?

After Reading

- Prompt the child to think more. Ask: What was life like in ancient Rome? What more would you like to learn about this time period?

Grasshopper Books are published by Jump!
5357 Penn Avenue South
Minneapolis, MN 55419
www.jumplibrary.com

Copyright © 2025 Jump! International copyright reserved in all countries. No part of this book may be reproduced in any form without written permission from the publisher.

Library of Congress Cataloging-in-Publication Data

Names: Havemeyer, Janie, author.
Samaniego, César, 1975- illustrator.
Title: A day in ancient Rome / by Janie Havemeyer; illustrated by Cesar Samaniego.
Description: Minneapolis, MN: Jump!, Inc., 2025.
Series: Ancient civilizations | Includes index.
Audience: Ages 7-10
Identifiers: LCCN 2024028458 (print)
LCCN 2024028459 (ebook)
ISBN 9798892134866 (hardcover)
ISBN 9798892134873 (paperback)
ISBN 9798892134880 (ebook)
Subjects: LCSH: Rome–Civilization–Juvenile literature.
Classification: LCC DG77 .H348 2025 (print)
LCC DG77 (ebook)
DDC 937–dc23/eng/20240802
LC record available at https://lccn.loc.gov/2024028458
LC ebook record available at https://lccn.loc.gov/2024028459

Editor: Alyssa Sorenson
Direction and Layout: Anna Peterson
Illustrator: Cesar Samaniego
Content Consultant: David Potter, Francis W. Kelsey Collegiate Professor of Greek and Roman History, University of Michigan

Printed in the United States of America at Corporate Graphics in North Mankato, Minnesota.

Table of Contents

Gladiators and Games	4
Ancient Rome Timeline	22
Map of Ancient Rome	23
To Learn More	23
Glossary	24
Index	24

Gladiators and Games

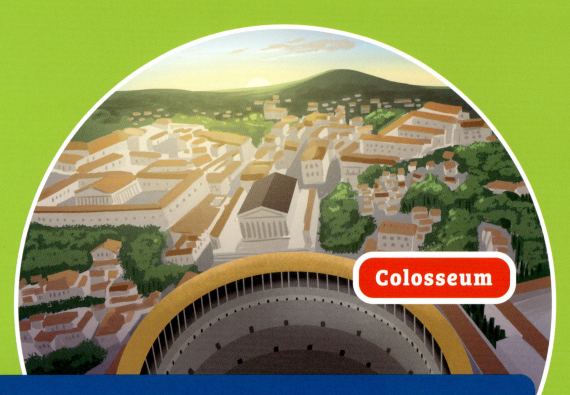

Colosseum

It is summer in the year 99. The Sun rises over Rome. This is the **capital** of the mighty Roman **Empire**. Games will be held at the Colosseum later today.

But first, work must get done. In the country, a farmer cuts wheat in his field. His wife milks the cow. His daughter waters the garden.

In the city, **senators** wear togas. They listen to **Emperor** Trajan. He wants to build a new **aqueduct**. It will bring drinking and bath water to Rome. Many senators agree a new aqueduct is a good idea!

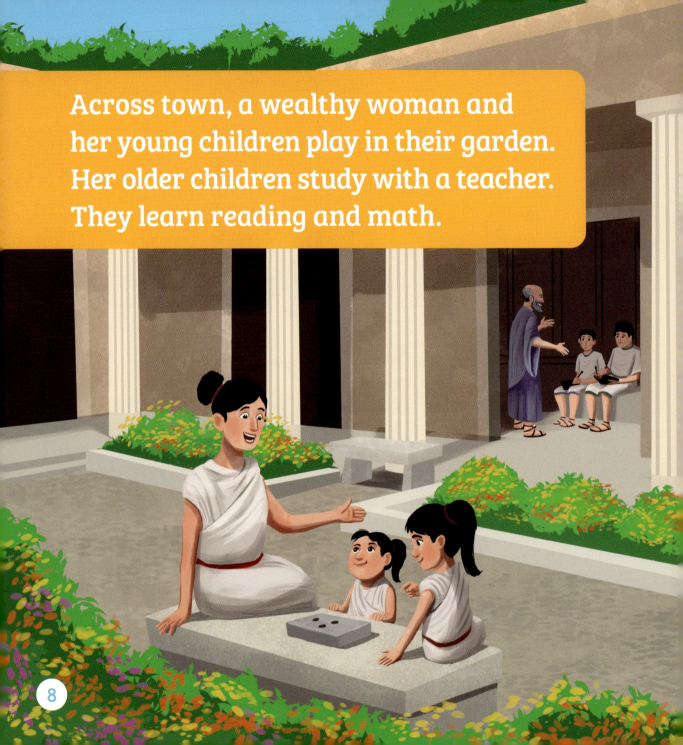

Across town, a wealthy woman and her young children play in their garden. Her older children study with a teacher. They learn reading and math.

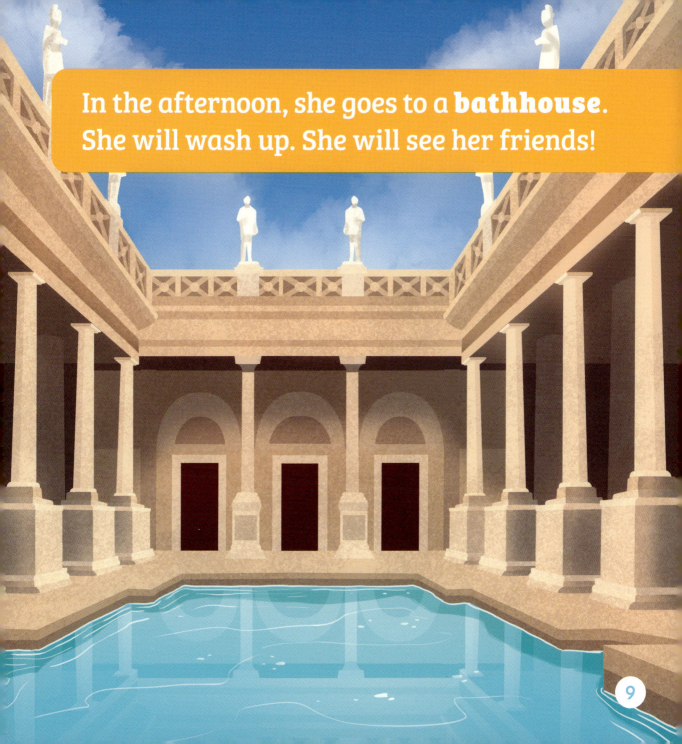

In the afternoon, she goes to a **bathhouse**. She will wash up. She will see her friends!

People visit shops. They buy clothing and jewelry. They buy fresh bread at the bakery.

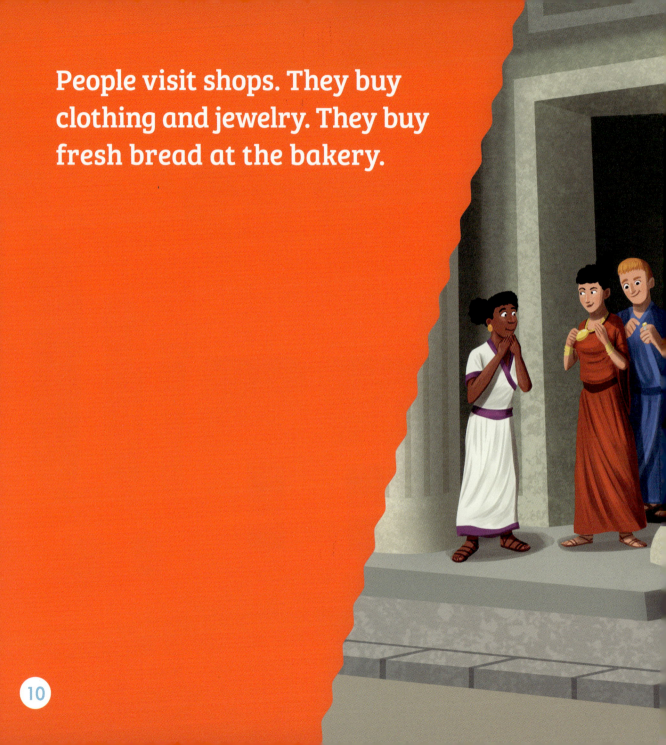

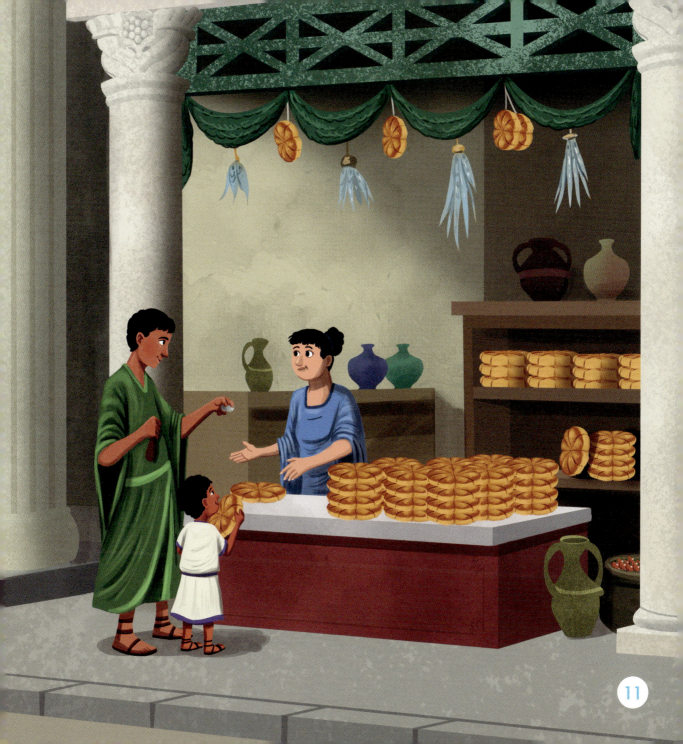

An excited crowd gathers around a lake. There is a fake ship battle! People sail. They try to sink each other's ships!

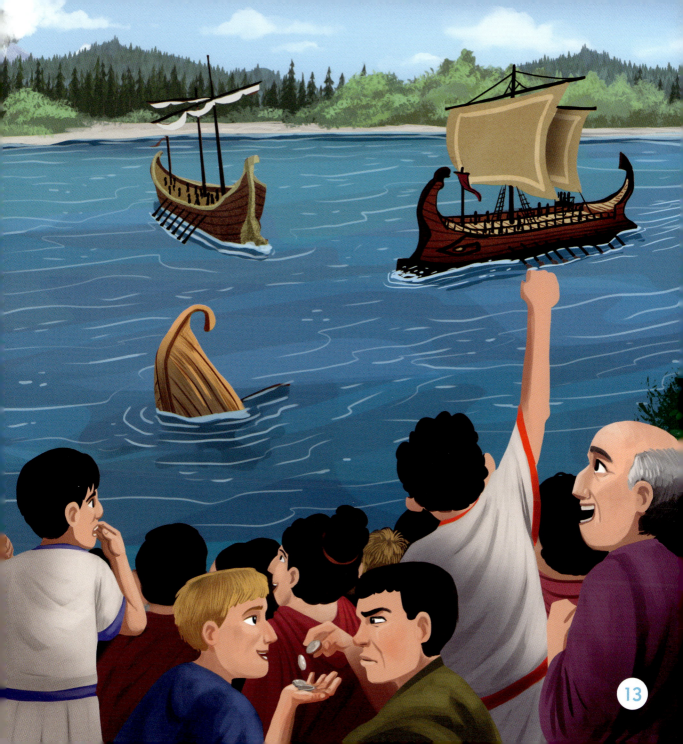

There is a battle at the Colosseum, too. Thousands of people come to watch.

Two **gladiators** face off. One swings his sword. But he gets caught in a net! He wiggles free. The crowd cheers!

Afterward, some people go to the theater. There is another performance to watch. It is a **comedy**. Actors wear masks. They sing and dance on a stage. The audience laughs and claps.

All day long, people visit **temples**. They ask the **gods** for help. They hope for good health. They pray that their friends will return safely from war. People place coins and small statues inside the temples. These are gifts for the gods.

At sunset, it is time for dinner. A family invites friends over. Everyone eats meat and vegetables with olive oil. They talk and listen to music. It has been a busy day in ancient Rome!

Ancient Rome Timeline

What are some important events in the Roman Empire's history? Take a look!

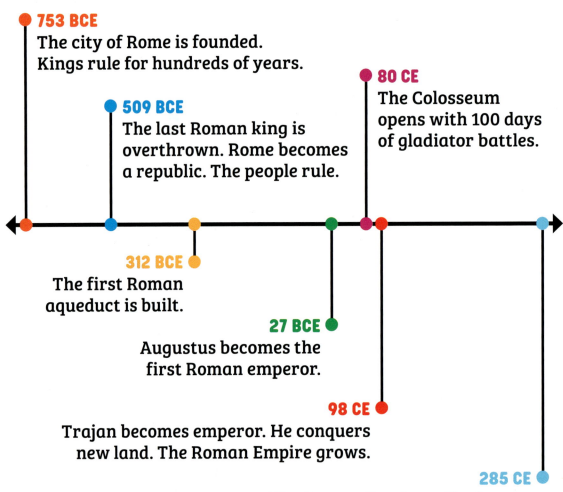

- **753 BCE** — The city of Rome is founded. Kings rule for hundreds of years.
- **509 BCE** — The last Roman king is overthrown. Rome becomes a republic. The people rule.
- **312 BCE** — The first Roman aqueduct is built.
- **27 BCE** — Augustus becomes the first Roman emperor.
- **80 CE** — The Colosseum opens with 100 days of gladiator battles.
- **98 CE** — Trajan becomes emperor. He conquers new land. The Roman Empire grows.
- **285 CE** — The Roman Empire splits in two.

22

Map of Ancient Rome

Take a look at the Roman Empire during Emperor Trajan's rule.

To Learn More

Finding more information is as easy as 1, 2, 3.

❶ Go to www.factsurfer.com
❷ Enter "**ancientRome**" into the search box.
❸ Choose your book to see a list of websites.

23

Glossary

aqueduct: A structure that carries water across land to a city.

bathhouse: A public building in which people bathe.

capital: The city in a country where the government is based.

comedy: A performance that is funny.

emperor: A male ruler of an empire.

empire: A group of countries or states that have the same ruler.

gladiators: Men in ancient Rome who fought other men or wild animals to provide entertainment.

gods: Beings that are worshipped and are believed to have special powers over nature and life.

senators: Citizens who advise and help govern.

temples: Buildings in which gods are worshipped.

Index

aqueduct 6

Colosseum 4, 14

gladiators 15

gods 18

Roman Empire 4

Rome 4, 6, 20

senators 6

temples 18

theater 16

togas 6

Trajan 6

wheat 5